WILDLIFE SURVIVAL

Gorillas
in DANGER

by Helen Orme

Consultant: Dr. Annette Lanjouw
Director of the International Gorilla Conservation Program

BEARPORT
PUBLISHING

New York, New York

Credits
Corbis: 15. Digital Vision: 4–5, 6–7, 8–9, 10–11, 12–13, 14, 18–19, 20, 22–23, 24–25, 26–27, 28–29, 30–31, 32. FLPA: OFC, 20–21. Nature Picture Library: 16–17, 18. Every effort has been made to trace the copyright holders, and we apologize in advance for any unintentional omissions. We would be pleased to insert the appropriate acknowledgments in any subsequent edition of this publication.

Library of Congress Cataloging-in-Publication Data

Orme, Helen.
  Gorillas in danger / by Helen Orme.
      p. cm. — (Wildlife survival)
  Includes index.
  ISBN-13: 978-1-59716-261-6 (library binding)
  ISBN-10: 1-59716-261-2 (library binding)
  ISBN-13: 978-1-59716-289-0 (pbk.)
  ISBN-10: 1-59716-289-2 (pbk.)
  1. Gorilla—Juvenile literature. I. Title. II. Series.

  QL737.P96O725 2007
  599.884—dc22
                                      2006012846

For more information, write to Bearport Publishing Company, Inc., 101 Fifth Avenue, Suite 6R, New York, New York 10003. Printed in the United States of America.

10 9 8 7 6 5 4 3 2 1

The Wildlife Survival series was originally developed by ticktock Media Ltd.

Table of Contents

Rare Animals

There are only about 700 mountain gorillas left in the world. They live in thick, misty **rain forests** high up in the mountains of Africa. Some of the mountains are **dormant** volcanoes.

About half of all mountain gorillas live on the slopes of the Virunga volcanoes in Africa.

Mountain gorillas are one of the rarest animals in the world.

Young Mountain Gorillas

After a gorilla is born, the mother holds the baby close to her chest for the first few months. As the baby gets older, the mother begins to carry the young gorilla on her back.

When gorillas are about one year old, they start to climb trees and play on their own. However, they never stray far from their mothers.

A baby gorilla weighs about five pounds (2 kg) when it's born.

Families

Gorillas live in family groups. The groups are made up of a few male and female adults. There are also several young gorillas and some babies.

Adult male gorillas are called silverbacks because they have silver-colored fur on their backs. Each family has a silverback as a leader to protect the group.

Silverbacks keep other animals away by acting tough. They stand on their back legs and beat their chests.

Looking for Food

Gorillas spend their day moving through the forest **foraging** for food. They eat stinging nettles, bamboo thistles, and other leafy plants.

Although they're mainly **vegetarians**, these **apes** sometimes look for worms, grubs, and ants. Adult gorillas can eat up to 66 pounds (30 kg) of food each day.

Baby gorillas drink their mothers' milk until they are about two years old.

Gorillas have strong jaws and teeth for grinding up tough plant stalks.

Difficult Times

About 100 years ago, people living outside of Africa discovered the mountain gorillas. Once people found out about these animals, they came to Africa and started hunting them.

Soon there weren't many gorillas left. To help save them, laws were passed to keep the animals safe. Hunting became **illegal**. The areas where gorillas lived were turned into **protected parks**.

Gorillas move around a lot. They never spend more than one night in the same place.

More Trouble

For a while, the new laws made life better for the gorillas. Then in 1990, a terrible war broke out in Africa. People tried to escape by hiding in the mountains. Some gorillas caught human diseases and died.

Other people who lived near the protected parks decided they needed more land for farming and firewood. They cut down the trees in the parks, destroying the gorillas' **habitat**. These apes had no place to live. Many of them died.

The trees that people cut down in the protected parks were used for fuel.

Poachers

Poaching is another problem the mountain gorillas face. Usually the poachers hunt antelopes or pigs. Yet the **snares** they use to catch their **prey** sometimes trap gorillas. They are often injured by the traps. Some die from wounds. Others cannot free themselves from the traps and starve to death.

The gorillas' only real enemy is people.

*Park rangers carry away the body of a
dead gorilla that was caught in a snare.*

People Who Help

Life is difficult for mountain gorillas. However, there are people who can help them. **Park rangers** patrol the forests. If they find an animal that is sick or in trouble, it can get help.

The mountain gorillas also have their own **veterinarians**. These people go into the forests to treat the gorillas with medicine. They can even perform operations.

Dian Fossey was a **zoologist** who studied the behavior of wild gorillas for about 20 years.

*Park rangers check
on a sick gorilla.*

Visiting the Gorillas

These days, people from around the world are allowed to visit the gorillas. This helps bring money and jobs to the people who live nearby. So, it's important to the local people to protect the gorillas.

Visitors are allowed to stay with the animals for only one hour. They can't get closer than 23 feet (7 m). This distance keeps the gorillas from getting human diseases.

Bwindi, in Uganda, is the most popular gorilla park for **tourists**.

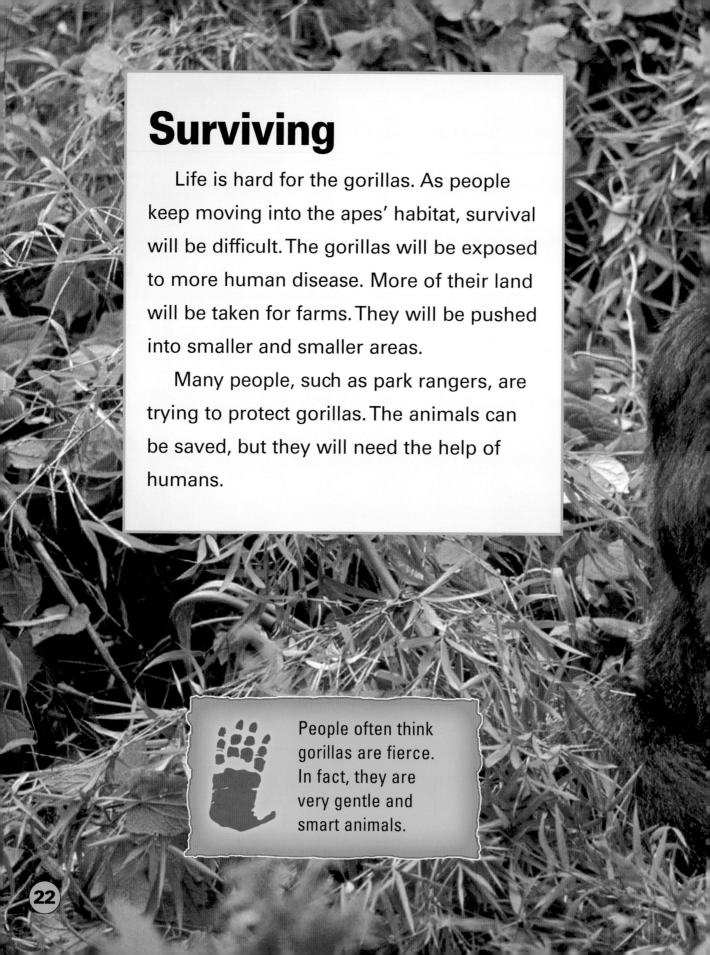

Surviving

Life is hard for the gorillas. As people keep moving into the apes' habitat, survival will be difficult. The gorillas will be exposed to more human disease. More of their land will be taken for farms. They will be pushed into smaller and smaller areas.

Many people, such as park rangers, are trying to protect gorillas. The animals can be saved, but they will need the help of humans.

People often think gorillas are fierce. In fact, they are very gentle and smart animals.

Where Do Mountain Gorillas Live?

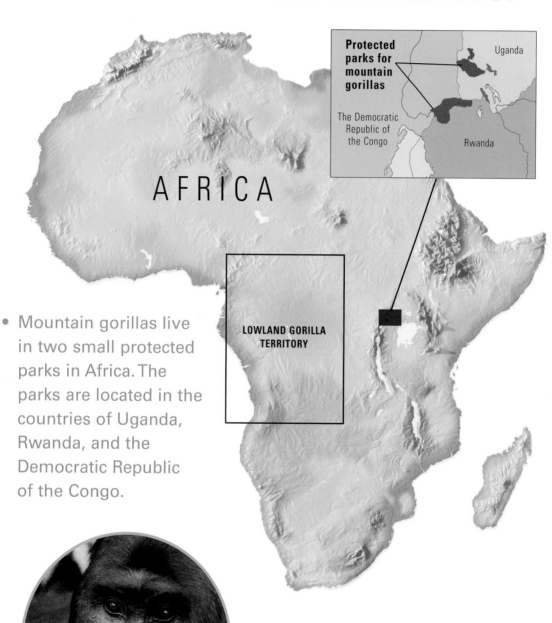

Protected
parks for
mountain
gorillas

Uganda

The Democratic
Republic of
the Congo

Rwanda

AFRICA

LOWLAND GORILLA
TERRITORY

- Mountain gorillas live in two small protected parks in Africa. The parks are located in the countries of Uganda, Rwanda, and the Democratic Republic of the Congo.

- Lowland gorillas, another type of endangered gorilla, also live in Africa.

24

Mountain Gorilla Bodies

- Gorillas are the largest of all apes.
- When gorillas walk on all fours, they're about 3 feet (1 m) tall.

Male
Weight: up to 441 pounds (200 kg)
Height: 6 feet (1.8 m)

Female
Weight: up to 198 pounds (90 kg)
Height: 5 feet (1.5 m)

More About Family Life

- Families are made up of about 5 to 30 gorillas.

- The young males usually leave the group when they're about 11 years old. By the time they're 15 years old, they usually have their own family group.

- Female gorillas stay with the family until they're about 8 years old. At that time, they usually join a new group.

- At night, gorillas sleep in nests that are made from leaves and branches. These beds are either on the ground or up in a tree.

- Grooming is a very important part of a gorilla's daily life. The animals clean one another's fur and remove insects.

- In the wild, gorillas live for 30 to 40 years.

More About Gorilla Food

- Mountain gorillas spend most of their day looking for food. They may travel between 1 to 2 miles (2 to 3 km) in search of something to eat.

- Gorillas eat about 142 different types of plants, including herbs and fruits.

- Gorillas don't have to drink water. They get all they need from eating plants.

More About Gorillas in Danger

- All kinds of gorillas, not just mountain gorillas, are in danger because of poaching and habitat loss.

How many gorillas are left?	
Type of Gorilla	**Population**
Mountain Gorilla	700
Eastern Lowland Gorilla	7,000
Western Lowland Gorilla	10,000

- Many zoos are helping to protect lowland gorillas by taking them in. Mountain gorillas cannot be protected in this way. They can't survive in zoos.

Conservation

- Due to **conservation**, the number of mountain gorillas is slowly beginning to increase.

- Saving the mountain gorillas' habitat is not just a good thing for the gorillas. It also helps all the other plants and animals that live in the rain forests.

- To save the gorillas, it's important to help the people who live near them. Conservationists are showing these people how to raise rabbits and goats. This practice will stop them from using snares to catch wild animals, which can injure or kill gorillas.

How to Help

Conservation is everyone's job. There are many ways to help mountain gorillas:

- Learn more about these animals. Then teach others at school about the importance of helping them.

- Help an organization, such as the African Wildlife Foundation (AWF) (www.awf.org). Groups such as this one raise money to pay for conservation work. To help the AWF or another conservation group, have a yard sale. Sell old clothes, toys, and books. Then donate the money that is made to the group.

- Be a good conservationist. Visit www.worldwildlife.org/act/action.cfm for tips on how to help take care of the world.

Visit these Web sites for more information on mountain gorillas and how to help them:

www.awf.org/wildlives/149
www.gorillafund.org
www.mountaingorillas.org
www.worldwildlife.org/gorillas/

Glossary

apes (APES) a group of mammals that includes chimpanzees, gorillas, and orangutans

conservation (*kon*-sur-VAY-shuhn) the protection of wildlife, forests, and natural resources

dormant (DOR-muhnt) not active, but could be in the future

foraging (FOR-ij-ing) looking for food in the wild

habitat (HAB-uh-tat) a place in the wild where an animal or plant lives

illegal (i-LEE-guhl) against the law

park rangers (PARK RAYN-jurz) people who look after parks and forests and the animals that live there

poaching (POHCH-ing) hunting illegally on someone else's land

prey (PRAY) animals that are hunted by other animals for food

protected parks (pruh-TEK-tid PARKS) areas where hunting animals or cutting down trees is against the law

rain forests (RAYN FOR-ists) warm, wet places where lots of trees and plants grow

snares (SNAIRZ) traps made from wire

tourists (TOOR-ists) people who are traveling on vacation

vegetarians (*vej*-uh-TAIR-ee-uhnz) people or animals who only eat plants or dairy products and don't eat meat

veterinarians (*vet*-ur-uh-NAIR-ee-uhnz) doctors who treat sick or injured animals

zoologist (zoh-OL-uh-jist) a person who studies animal life

Index